21st
Century
Skills Library

COOL CAREERS

HEAVY EQUIPMENT OPERATOR

NANCY ROBINSON MASTERS

Published in the United States of America by
Cherry Lake Publishing, Ann Arbor, Michigan
www.cherrylakepublishing.com

Content Adviser
Louis Teel, Professor of Heavy Equipment, Central Arizona College

Credits
Photos: Cover and pages 1 and 23, ©Stanislav Komogorov/Shutterstock, Inc.;
page 4, ©iStockphoto.com/Pacificenterprise; page 6, ©iStockphoto.com/Andyqwe;
page 9, ©Symbiot/Shutterstock, Inc.; page 10, ©Ambient Ideas/Shutterstock,
Inc.; page 12, ©iStockphoto.com/eliandric; page 14, ©JinYoung Lee/Shutterstock,
Inc.; page 17, ©Picsfive/Shutterstock, Inc.; page 18, ©iStockphoto.com/lisafx;
page 20, ©Anton Foltin/Shutterstock, Inc.; page 23, ©Stanislav Komogorov/
Shutterstock, Inc.; page 24, ©inginsh/Shutterstock, Inc.; page 27, ©Andrejs
Pidjass/Shutterstock, Inc.; page 28, ©Leo/Shutterstock, Inc.

Library of Congress Cataloging-in-Publication Data
Masters, Nancy Robinson.
  Heavy equipment operator/by Nancy Robinson Masters.
      p. cm.—(Cool careers)
  Includes bibliographical references and index.
  ISBN-13: 978-1-60279-941-7 (lib. bdg.)
  ISBN-10: 1-60279-941-5 (lib. bdg.)
  1. Building—Vocational guidance—Juvenile literature. 2. Construction
equipment—Juvenile literature. 3. Earthwork—Vocational guidance—Juvenile
literature. 4. Earthmoving machinery operators—Juvenile literature.
I. Title. II. Series.
  TH159.M37 2010
  690.023—dc22   2010003015

Cherry Lake Publishing would like to acknowledge
the work of The Partnership for 21st Century Skills.
Please visit *www.21stcenturyskills.org* for more information.

Printed in the United States of America
Corporate Graphics Inc.
July 2010
CLFA07

TABLE OF CONTENTS

CHAPTER ONE
THE BIG PICTURE

Victor grabbed his backpack. He tossed the empty milk carton into the kitchen trash. He did not want to miss the school bus. It usually stops in front of Victor's house each

Heavy equipment operators control tall cranes needed to build hospitals and other large buildings.

weekday morning. But starting today, things would be different. Construction projects had started at the hospital down the street. This construction work will block traffic. Only bulldozers and other large machines will be allowed on the road. Victor and his sister Lana will have to walk to the end of the road to board the bus.

"Today is trash day," his mother reminded. "But the truck can't come down our road, Victor. You need to take the trash to the dumpster at Memorial Hospital. We can use its dumpster during construction. Drop the bag off on your way to the bus."

"I'll help," Lana offered. She tied the trash sack closed.

As Victor and Lana made their way to the dumpster, they saw many heavy equipment operators at work inside the fence around the hospital parking lot. Heavy equipment operators are people who run large, powerful machinery. The kids spotted a 150-foot (45.7 meter) tall crane. It lifted huge beams of steel to workers on top of the hospital. A backhoe dug ditches beside the road. It used a special digging bucket. New water pipes will be placed in the ditch. A pile driver machine hammered long beams of steel deep into the ground. These beams will help form the foundation of a new parking garage.

"Good thing these trash dumpsters are outside the construction area!" Lana yelled. Victor could barely hear her above the noise of the engines. "It wouldn't be safe for us to go inside the fence."

Lana handed Victor the sack of trash to place inside the dumpster. "Think of how many trash sacks a hospital fills each day," she said.

Lana waved to a woman driving a dump truck. The driver waved back. She was wearing a hard hat, gloves, and dust mask.

Victor closed the lid of the dumpster. He watched the backhoe operator through the fence. The operator used the

One operator can move more dirt with a powerful digging machine than many workers can move using hand shovels.

backhoe's bucket to dig dirt out of the ditch. Then the front loader on the backhoe scooped up the dirt. It dropped the dirt into the dump truck.

Victor leaned close to his sister's ear. "Remember when it took me all day to fill the flower boxes with dirt at our house? Can you imagine how much time it would take for me to fill a whole truck?"

Lana looked at her watch. The school bus would be arriving any minute. Victor was still watching the backhoe.

"It would be so cool to operate those powerful machines," he said. Victor did not want to leave.

Lana grabbed his arm. "Here comes the bus!"

■   ■   ■

What were the first construction tools? Sticks and stones were used to clear paths and build bridges. Then, people began developing simple machines. These included pulleys and levers. They were used to construct buildings. By the 15th century, tools and simple machines were used to build many things. Examples include castles and churches. Humans and animals provided the power for running some early machines.

Jump forward several centuries. Steam-powered machines began to replace human and animal power. This was the beginning of the **Industrial Revolution**. The Otis Steam

Shovel was built in 1835. It was the first piece of engine-powered heavy equipment machinery. It ran on train tracks. Its shovel could be moved to dig on either side of the tracks.

21ST CENTURY CONTENT

Heavy equipment isn't just used at construction sites. The Energy Wood Harvester works inside forests. It gathers leftover trees and limbs. They are known as "slash." It bundles them into logs. Each bundle contains as much energy as half a barrel of oil. Removing the slash also helps protect forests from fire and insect damage. Operators of heavy equipment in the 21st century play an important part in saving energy and protecting the environment.

The term *horsepower* started being used as a measurement of energy. Horsepower compared the power of the steam engine to the power of horses. Equipment powered by steam engines changed how people worked and lived.

Heavy equipment improved in many ways in the 20th century. Electric and gasoline engines were designed.

An operator uses equipment to move a load of logs that will be made into enough lumber to build a house!

Rolling tracks replaced wheels on some equipment. These tracks made it possible for equipment to work over rough land. Why might that be important? Think of areas where there are no roads. Tracks also made it possible to operate larger, more powerful equipment. In the 1930s, companies such as Caterpillar Tractor Company began making heavy equipment with **diesel engines**. These engines were soon used to power most heavy equipment.

Can you find the cabs where the workers sit and operate the cranes?

More advances were made near the end of the century. Companies began adding computer features to heavy equipment. They added communications technology, too. This made the operator's job faster, easier, and safer. Computers make it possible to provide instructions instantly on a screen. People don't have to shout above noisy engines. They also don't have to stop working in order to communicate.

Today, heavy equipment operators use even more technology. This technology helps them build roads. It helps them drill for oil, dig mines, tear down buildings, and much more.

Digital controls and Global Positioning System (GPS) features are very helpful. They allow operators to position equipment with the touch of a finger. Crane operators use GPS to precisely position beams on top of buildings. Backhoe operators use GPS to dig to exact depths. This technology makes it easier for heavy equipment operators to be successful.

Older heavy equipment may not have digital and computer technology. It is still used around the world, though. Users of this equipment need excellent hand and foot control. They must have good vision, too.

Will Victor choose a career as a heavy equipment operator? If he does, he can count on having an exciting future.

CHAPTER TWO
ALL IN A DAY'S WORK

Roy Knowles needs a flashlight to begin his workday at the Abilene Environmental **Landfill**. He uses it to carefully inspect graders and other heavy equipment.

Heavy equipment operators are responsible for checking their equipment carefully before they start work.

More than 200 tons (181.4 metric tons) of trash arrive at the landfill each day. The machines spread, sort, compact, and cover the trash.

Roy looks for leaks from special hoses. He also checks for broken electrical wires. He makes sure the fuel and oil tanks are full. Roy knows his equipment well. He can fix many problems. What if he finds an equipment problem he cannot fix? He reports it to a mechanic.

A new bulldozer costs roughly $500,000. A new compactor costs $750,000. Taking good care of this expensive equipment is important. It's a big part of an equipment operator's job.

Roy has been a heavy equipment operator since graduating from high school. He first worked with his father in the road construction business. Roy later owned an asphalt paving business. He learned how to operate water trucks, asphalt spreaders, and graders.

Roy loves working outside. He decided years ago that he wanted to build something to help protect the environment. His skills as a heavy equipment operator proved to be very useful. He knew that the equipment he used to build roads could also be used to build a landfill. He purchased 260 acres (105.2 hectares) of unused land near Abilene, Texas.

The landfill site has to meet federal, state, and local **Environmental Protection Agency** (EPA) rules. Roy spent more than a year making sure his site met the rules. He also spent time training workers to run the machinery.

After checking the equipment, Roy meets with his employees. This takes place before the trucks that bring trash begin arriving at the landfill. This morning, everyone is planning a tour for a group of young students. The kids will visit the landfill the next day. The tour will help the students understand how the landfill works. The trash is buried in a special way. That way, it will not pollute the soil or

Large amounts of trash are dumped in landfills every day.

nearby water. Roy and his team will also explain to the students how burning trash pollutes the air.

This morning, the employees also watch a DVD. It is from the **Occupational Safety & Health Administration** (OSHA). The DVD explains new safety rules for heavy equipment operators at environmental landfills.

LEARNING & INNOVATION SKILLS

Landfills combine, compact, and cover trash. The landfill in Staten Island, New York, was once the largest landfill in the world. The landfill has since been closed. Construction has begun to turn the area into a park. Think about the different kinds of heavy equipment that were used to build this gigantic landfill. What kinds of heavy equipment might operators use to build the park?

"Working safely is for your protection," Roy tells the operators. "It also helps protect equipment and other workers," he explains.

Human hands don't touch the trash after it arrives at the landfill. A grader operator spreads the trash. That way, it can be examined. Special equipment removes any unsafe waste. This will be sent to a different location for safe disposal. Recyclable items are also removed. Then the compactor operator moves the spiked roller across the trash. The trash gets pressed into tiny pieces. Once compacted, a sack of trash would fit into one finger of a glove.

Today, Roy will operate the bulldozer. It will push all of the compacted trash into a pit that is 40 feet (12.2 m) deep. It will be covered with layers of dirt and special plastic. The plastic is very strong. Nothing can leak into or out of the landfill.

Workers at an environmental landfill must wear safety gear. This includes work boots and hard hats.

Listening to music is not allowed while running equipment. Neither is chatting on cell phones or texting. "A heavy equipment operator must be totally focused on doing the job," Roy explains.

All of the trash that comes in during the day is compacted and covered. Roy does not leave the landfill until this is done.

What does Roy like most about his job? "I am building something that is protecting our soil, water, and air today and for the future. When this landfill is full, it will be covered with trees, grass, and flowers. Kids will be able to safely ride bicycles or play soccer here."

Soil compactors are just one kind of equipment used at landfills.

CHAPTER THREE

BECOMING A HEAVY EQUIPMENT OPERATOR

C onstruction is a large industry in the United States. There will always be a need for workers with the skills

Heavy equipment operators learn much of what they need to know from more experienced operators.

to operate heavy equipment. **Developing countries** also offer opportunities for jobs. These countries need roads, bridges, dams, and buildings.

LIFE & CAREER SKILLS

The Caterpillar D9 is a 464-horsepower bulldozer. It has a hollow steel blade. It weighs 52.8 tons (47.9 MT). Operators use D9s and other Caterpillar equipment to clear and help rebuild areas after natural disasters. Getting heavy equipment to locations after disasters can be very difficult. Can you think of some reasons why?

You do not need a college degree to be a heavy equipment operator. It is easier, however, to find a job if you have a training course certificate or degree. Hands-on training with an experienced heavy equipment operator is the best way to gain the knowledge needed for the job.

Many colleges and trade schools offer courses and programs on heavy equipment operation. Most manufacturers provide training on how to operate the equipment they produce. Gaining skills takes time, patience, and a lot of practice.

Workers usually start by operating lighter equipment. This includes trucks. Then they can move on to heavy equipment such as bulldozers or graders.

Less than 1 out of 10 heavy equipment operators are women. Organizations are working to increase that number. One example is the National Association of Women in Construction (NAWIC).

It takes an experienced heavy equipment operator to use larger, more powerful machines such as graders.

Heavy equipment operators earn above average salaries. The exact amount often depends on their skills and experience. Workers can earn between roughly $13.00 and $33.00 per hour. Annual earnings may be lower than the hourly rates suggest. The number of hours worked might be limited. One reason is if there is a lot of bad weather in an area.

Heavy equipment operators may belong to trade unions. They may also work for companies or work for themselves. They must go where the work is. This may include faraway places. It may also mean going where earthquakes, floods, or other natural disasters have occurred.

Is a job as a heavy equipment operator right for you? To become an operator in the United States, you should

- graduate from high school;
- have a driver's license;
- enjoy being outdoors;
- have a strong interest in machines;
- like to solve problems;
- know how to prepare reports and keep records;
- be willing to get up early and work long hours;
- learn computer skills;
- be dependable;
- complete assignments on time;
- not mind getting dirty;
- respond quickly, but calmly, in emergencies;
- stay drug free and in good shape.

At school, you should enjoy math, science, and computers. You should also like social studies and physical education. Other important subjects are music, drama, and art. Do these last three surprise you? They shouldn't. Music strengthens listening skills. Drama improves language and memory skills. Art relates to design skills. These are all necessary skills for a heavy equipment operator.

Would you like to find out more about this career? There are many Web sites with pictures and videos of heavy equipment. Through your searches, you will likely find operators at work using all kinds of machinery.

Is there a construction or equipment company in your area? Ask an adult if these businesses offer tours. They may provide brochures or posters for you and your class.

What is the best way to learn about working as a heavy equipment operator? Talk to one! Ask your teacher to invite an operator to visit your class. Be ready with a list of questions to ask. Listening and asking questions will give you the inside scoop on this career.

Heavy equipment operators must stay focused on their jobs while working in a construction area.

CHAPTER FOUR
BUILDING THE FUTURE

Approximately 470,000 men and women worked as heavy equipment operators in the United States in 2008.

Knowing how to work as a part of a team is an important skill for a heavy equipment operator.

The U.S. Department of Labor predicts that at least 50,000 more will be needed by 2018.

21ST CENTURY CONTENT

Heavy equipment operators work in the air as well as on the ground. Helicopter pilots fly aircraft such as the Erickson S-64 Aircrane. This huge helicopter can lift as much as 25,000 pounds (11,339.8 kilograms)! It can place heavy equipment, such as large air conditioning units, on the tops of tall buildings. Helicopters can work in areas that are too difficult for ground equipment to reach. More helicopter pilots will be needed as heavy equipment operators in the sky in the 21st century.

What will heavy equipment operators do in the future? They will do many of the same things they do today. They'll build and repair roads, highways, and railroads. They'll help build airports, mines, dams, and bridges. They'll also help build systems for electricity, natural gas, and water.

They will be doing these jobs with equipment made of lighter-weight materials. The engines in the equipment may use fuel made from products other than oil. These machines will do less damage to the environment. They'll provide more safety for workers, too.

Operators will also help scientists learn new things about Earth. For example, heavy equipment operators use track vehicles in Antarctica. They bring scientists and supplies across large areas of ice to sites where research is being done. The scientists could not reach these sites without this equipment.

Think about technology that is in use today. One example is built-in laser systems for guiding operators. This technology will continue to improve in the years to come. Lasers send a focused beam of light. Future laser systems will make it possible for one grader operator to spread dirt more evenly across wider areas.

Some equipment makers are doing research on solar-powered equipment. Solar power would be helpful to operators working in areas damaged by natural disasters. It would also reduce the amount of air pollution created from burning fuels such as oil and gas.

A rover is a special vehicle that explores the surface of another planet. The Mars rovers are a good example of the heavy equipment of the future. The rovers are powered by solar panels. They are equipped with **robotic arms**,

At least 50,000 more heavy equipment operators will be needed by 2018.

buckets, cameras, and drills. Future heavy equipment operators may work from a central control area. They may use
computers to control many pieces of robotic machinery, each
doing a different job.

Saving time and fuel will be part of every operator's job.
So will reducing noise and air pollution.

The work of heavy equipment operators is and will
continue to be very important. These men and women use
technology, skills, and machinery to build a better world.

Will you become a heavy equipment operator someday?

SOME WELL-KNOWN HEAVY EQUIPMENT OPERATORS AND INNOVATORS

John Deere (1804–1886) was a blacksmith. He invented and marketed the first successful steel plow. Deere & Company became the leading manufacturer of farm equipment. Its products include tractors and harvesters used worldwide.

Benjamin Holt (1849–1920) built heavy equipment that moved on rolling tracks instead of wheels. Holt Manufacturing Company joined with C. L. Best Tractor Company in 1925 to form Caterpillar Tractor Company. It became the largest manufacturer of heavy equipment in the world.

R. G. LeTourneau (1888–1969) was an inventor. His earthmoving equipment changed the world during the 20th century. His ideas for building bigger and better equipment made him a leader in the heavy equipment industry. He provided equipment to developing countries and to areas damaged by natural disasters.

National Association of Women in Construction (1953–) was first organized by 16 women in the United States. NAWIC assists women who want to work in construction. It also supports those already working in the industry. NAWIC works with women in construction in Australia, Canada, New Zealand, South Africa, and the United States.

William S. Otis (1813–1839) invented the steam shovel in 1835. It was the first steam-powered piece of heavy equipment used to move earth.

GLOSSARY

developing countries (di-VEL-uhp-eeng KUHN-treez) countries in which most people have a lower standard of living than people in countries with higher incomes

diesel engines (DEE-suhl EN-jihnz) engines powered by a fuel called diesel oil

Environmental Protection Agency (en-vye-ruhn-MEN-tuhl proh-TEK-shuhn AY-juhn-see) an agency established by the U.S. government to protect the environment

Industrial Revolution (in-DUHSS-tree-uhl rev-uh-LOO-shuhn) a period of change in which machines began replacing human labor to produce goods or do work

landfill (LAND-fil) a place where trash is buried

Occupational Safety & Health Administration (ok-yuh-PAY-shuhn-uhl SAYF-tee AND HELTH ad-min-ih-STRAY-shuhn) an agency established by the U.S. government to protect the health and safety of workers

robotic arms (roh-BOT-ik ARMZ) parts of a machine that work like human arms to control other machines or tools

FOR MORE INFORMATION

BOOKS

Abramson, Andra Serlin. *Heavy Equipment Up Close*. New York: Sterling, 2007.

Jennings, Terry. *Construction Vehicles*. Mankato, MN: Smart Apple Media, 2009.

WEB SITES

Deere & Company—John Deere: A Biography
www.deere.com/en_US/compinfo/history/johndeere.html
Find out more about John Deere.

Kikki's Workshop
www.kenkenkikki.jp/e_index2.html
Learn about different types of heavy equipment at this fun site.

INDEX

ABOUT THE AUTHOR

Nancy Robinson Masters is the author of more than 30 books and thousands of articles for magazines and newspapers. Her father and grandfather were both heavy equipment operators. She grew up on a farm in West Texas where she learned to operate farm and construction machinery before she learned how to drive a car. She now lives on a farm next to the airport runway she built with her husband, Bill Masters.